What Is Prayer?

Discussion:

Every day, you talk and listen. It's important to do both. Your friend has something funny to tell you. If you don't listen, you will miss it. You like to talk, too. You may want to talk about your puppy. You may want to ask your grandpa, "How old are you?"

Prayer is our human way of talking and listening to God. It is important to do both. You can sing or say the words of a prayer out loud — God loves to hear your voice and listens. You can also say a prayer in your heart — anytime, anywhere. You can pray, "Dear God, bless my day" so quietly that no one hears — except God. God loves your silent prayers, too.

God usually speaks in a special way — God speaks to your heart. God has messages just for you. God wants you to know that you are good and are loved. Don't worry. Don't be afraid. Like a good friend, God wants to talk and always listens.

Activity: Tell what the children in the pictures might be talking about.

W9-APS-890

Why Do We Pray?

"Thank you God."

"I said a prayer for you."

"I'm Sorry."

"Let's have fun."

Discussion:

We pray because we want God as our good friend. We talk to our friend. Then we listen carefully. Friendship needs this sharing. God wants to hear what you have to say. God wants to hear your heart speak.

There are many reasons to pray. Here are some more:
- to honor, praise, and thank God for the beauty and variety of God's wonderful world — the sun, moon, stars, flowers, trees, forests, birds, fish, animals, rivers, lakes, mountains, forests, snow, rain, and beautiful rainbows;
- to ask God's help when you are sick or someone you know needs special help;
- to tell God you are sorry when you have been unkind to one of God's other friends;
- to tell God about your life, today — God wants to hear from you when you feel happy or sad; calm or restless, and even when you feel strong or afraid; and
- to ask God's help to be kind and loving when you are with your family and friends.

Activity: Tell what you can talk to God about.

When Can We Pray?

Discussion:

We can pray anytime, day or night. We can pray at home, school, or church. We can pray indoors or outdoors. We can pray alone or with others. We can say memorized prayers (learned by heart), we can sing songs, or we can say silent prayers that come from the heart. God likes all of our prayers — anytime!

Activities: • Connect the dots to form a pathway from morning to night.
  • In the circle next to each picture, write the page number of a prayer in this book that you could say at each picture.

Prayer Positions

Discussion:

We can pray to God anywhere, anytime, and in many different positions. In church we say or sing prayers while standing, kneeling, and sitting. Walking or riding to school, we can say a silent prayer in our heart. At school we can gather in a circle with our classmates to say or sing a morning prayer song. At the dinner table we can stand or sit, fold our hands, or join hands with others to say a mealtime prayer. At bedtime we can kneel or lie in bed as we say a nighttime prayer.

Activities:
- Talk about a prayer that you could say at each picture.
- Color the pictures.

Family Prayer

God made us a family.

We need one another.
We help one another.
We love one another.
We forgive one another.

We play together.
We work together.
We celebrate together.
We praise God together.

Thank you, God,
for our special family.
Amen.

Activity: Draw your family.

Sign of the Cross

1. (Hands together)

2. In the name of the Father . . .

3. and of the Son . . .

4. and of the Holy. . .

5. Spirit.

6. Amen.

1. Join hands in preparation.
2. Lay the left hand on the breast, and with the extended right
   hand touch the forehead, saying: "In the name of the Father."
3. Touch the breast, saying: "and of the Son."
4. Touch the left shoulder, saying: "and of the Holy . . ."; then
5. the right shoulder, saying: "Spirit."
6. Finally, join hands and say: "Amen."

Discussion:

Upon entering the church, dip your fingertips into the holy water font and make the shape of a cross on yourself. This short prayer is called the *Sign of the Cross.* We bless ourselves with water to remind us that we were baptized with water and belong to God's family.

Activity: With the help of your teacher and/or parent(s) practice making the *Sign of the Cross.*

Morning Prayer

Good morning, dear God!

The

and

praise you!

The

and

praise you!

Thank you, God, for a bright new day.
Be with me as I wake and play.
Help me be my best for you today. Amen.

Activity: • Say this prayer by reading the words and naming the pictures.
          • Color the pictures.

Guardian Angel Prayer

Angel of God
My Guardian Dear,
Every Day
Be At My Side
To Guard And Protect
To Help And Guide.
Amen.

Discussion:

God's Word in the Bible and our Catholic faith teach us that God created angels and that although we can't see them, they exist. Angels have often served as messengers, like the angel Gabriel who was sent by God to tell Mary that she would become the mother of God's only Son, Jesus.

Angels are also God's special helpers in the world. Psalm 91 in the Bible tells us: *God assigns angels to guard people in all that they do.* (Cf. *Ps* 91:11) By assigning guardian angels to guide and watch over us, God shows love and concern for us. (Cf. CCC 328-336)

Activity: Color the pictures around the prayer.

Mealtime Prayer

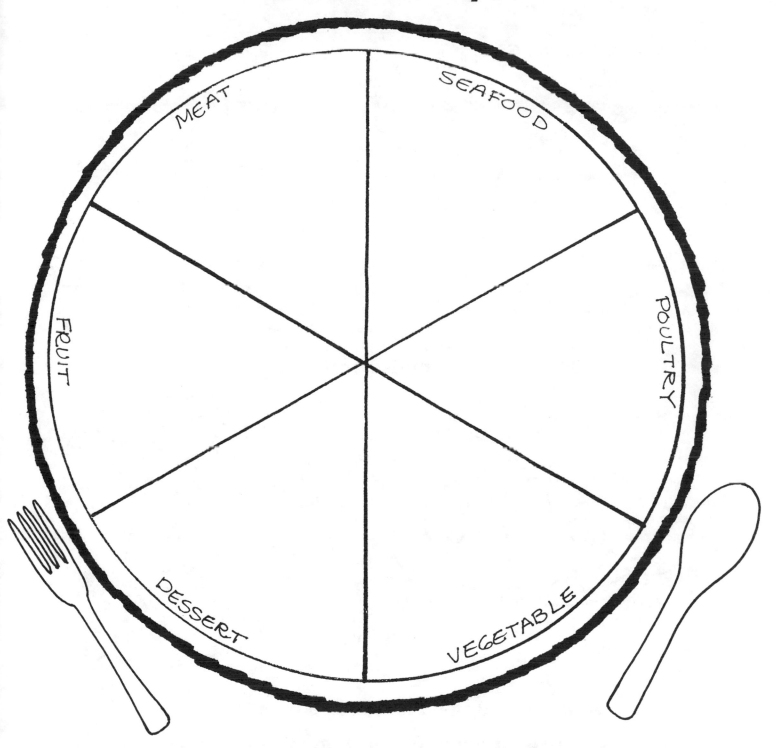

Bless us, O Lord, and these your gifts which we are about to receive from your goodness through Christ our Lord. Amen.

Activity: Draw and color your favorite foods in each of the six parts of the plate.

Nighttime Prayer

Good night, dear God!

The 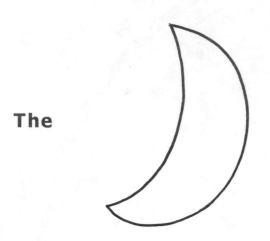 **and**

praise you!

The  **and**

praise you!

Thank you, dear God, for a wonderful day,

I had so much fun with my friends today.

I love you, dear God, and am happy to say,

Bless everyone who took care of me today. Amen.

Activity: • Say this prayer by reading the words and naming the pictures.
   • Color the pictures.

I'm Sorry Prayer

I'm sorry, dear God,

I made a mistake.

I hurt somebody's feelings.

I know that it was wrong.

It made my friend unhappy

and now my heart is hurting, too.

I want to be a better friend and

I want to be kind and helpful.

Dear God, you can help me to act better.

I know that's what you want,

and that's what I want, too.

Amen.

Happiness is saying, "I'm sorry!"

Activity: Complete the rainbow and color the pictures.

Classroom Prayer/Song

Dear God, Hear Your Little Children
Classroom Prayer

Joan E. Plum

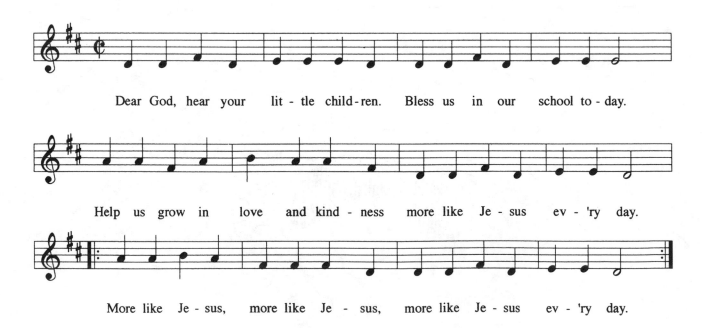

Dear God, hear your lit - tle child - ren. Bless us in our school to - day.

Help us grow in love and kind - ness more like Je - sus ev - 'ry day.

More like Je - sus, more like Je - sus, more like Je - sus ev - 'ry day.

Activities: • With the help of your teacher or parent(s), learn to say or sing this prayer.
• Color the picture.

Friendship Prayer

Dear God, thank you for showing your love for me by giving me friends. Please help me to learn how to show my love for them through playing and working together nicely, sharing, and being helpful to one another. Amen.

Activities: • Talk about what is happening in each picture.
• Color each picture.

Prayer for Grandparents

Dear God, please bless and always take care of my grandparents.

Through their care and understanding they have taught me
about your love and patience.

Through their encouragement and support they have made me
feel wanted and special.

Through their examples and faith, they have taught me about
trust and hope in you.

Through their stories and talks they have explained the past,
so that I might learn for my future.

Bless and protect my grandparents today and always, dear God.

Amen.

Activity: Color the flower bouquet.

Advent Prayers

On each of the four Sundays of Advent, gather with your family around an Advent wreath and light a candle on the wreath. The following prayers can be used:

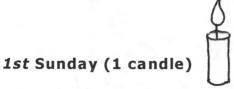

1st Sunday (1 candle)

Dear God, please bless this wreath and help our family to remember that Advent is a time to prepare for the celebration of Jesus' birthday. Amen.

2nd Sunday (2 candles)

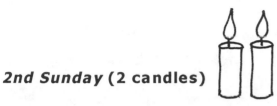

Dear God, as we decorate our home for Christmas, we think about the birth of your Son, Jesus. Help us to show love and kindness toward one another as we prepare to celebrate Christmas. Amen.

3rd Sunday (3 candles)

Dear God, Jesus' birthday celebration is very close. As we choose gifts for our family and friends, we stop to say, "Thank you, God, for Jesus — your gift to us." Amen.

4th Sunday (4 candles)

Dear God, it's almost Christmas. We are so excited! Please have Jesus' birthday celebration bring peace and joy to our family, friends, and to people everywhere. Amen.

Activity: After saying the Advent prayer each week, color a candle and flame.

Christmas Prayer

Dear God, I am happy that Jesus was born long ago.

You shared your love with us when you gave us Jesus.

Please help me to share my love with others, too. Amen.

Activity: • Draw a stable to protect Jesus, Mary, and Joseph.
• Color this Christmas scene.

Valentine Prayer

Dear God, thank you for wanting and loving me.

Thank you for my family who loves and takes care of me.

Thank you for my teacher who helps me to learn.

Thank you for my friends who play with me.

Thank you for helping me to show love

for others.

Thank you for a

Happy Valentine's Day.

Amen.

Discussion:

Many Christians honor the memory of St. Valentine, who loved God very much. This popular holiday is a good opportunity to celebrate love for family and friends. It is also a good day to remember the words of Jesus: *I give you a new commandment: love one another. As I have loved you, so love one another.* (Cf Jn 13:34) When Jesus gives us a *commandment,* it means he is asking us to do something. Jesus is telling us to show our love for one another through words and actions.

Activities: • Answer the following questions:
— Love is sharing; what can you share?
— Love is inviting someone to play; who could you invite to play?
— Love is taking turns; what toy can you take turns with?
— Love is helping your family; how could you help your family?
• Connect the dots to form a Valentine and then color the picture.

Easter Jelly Bean Prayer

- *Red* is for all the love Jesus showed us;

- *Purple* is for the sadness of his death;

- *Orange* is for the setting sun that faithful day;

- *Black* is for the nights Jesus spent in the tomb;

- *Yellow* is for the brightness of the Easter morning sun;

- *Pink* is for our joy — Jesus is alive!

- *White* is for the Easter candle — Jesus is our light!

- *Green* is for the hope and promise of new life in spring.

- A bag of jelly beans colorful and sweet

. . . is a reminder!

. . . is a prayer!

. . . is a special treat!

— Adapted from a folk prayer,
original author unknown.

Activity: Color the jelly beans to show your favorite flavors.

Vacation/Travel Prayer

Dear God, thank you for giving us vacation time to explore and enjoy your wonderful world. There are so many exciting places to see and people to visit. Be with us and protect us in our travel so that we can return home again safe and happy from our trip. Amen.

Activities: • Tell about your favorite trip. Include where you went and how you traveled.
• Color the pictures.

Glory and Praise Prayer

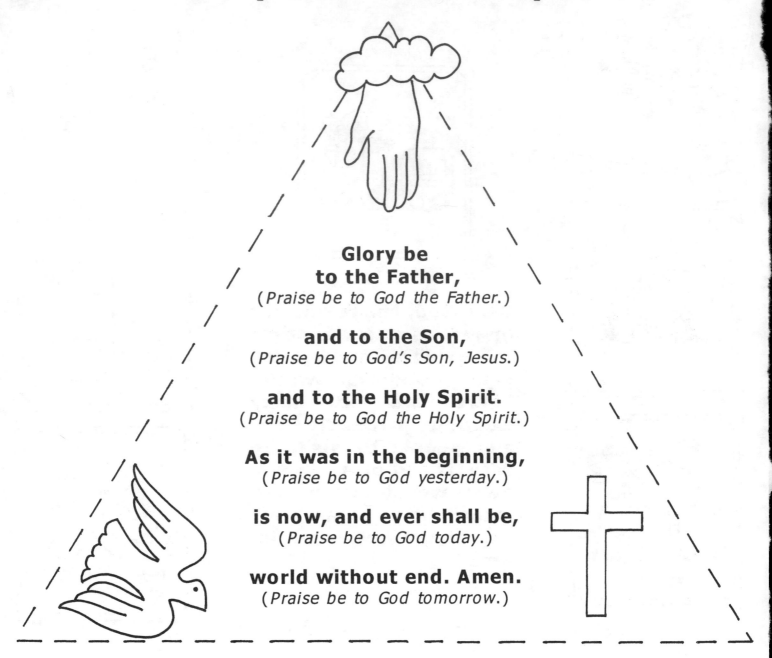

**Glory be
to the Father,**
(*Praise be to God the Father.*)

and to the Son,
(*Praise be to God's Son, Jesus.*)

and to the Holy Spirit.
(*Praise be to God the Holy Spirit.*)

As it was in the beginning,
(*Praise be to God yesterday.*)

is now, and ever shall be,
(*Praise be to God today.*)

world without end. Amen.
(*Praise be to God tomorrow.*)

Discussion:

This prayer refers to the three persons in One God — the Father, the Son (Jesus), and the Holy Spirit. This mystery of three persons in one God is called the **Trinity** and is represented by a triangle.

This short prayer of praise and faith in God is often said while making the *Sign of the Cross*. (See pg. 6.)

The Hand, Cross, and Dove in a triangle are symbols used in Christian art to represent God the Father, the Son (Jesus), and the Holy Spirit.

Activities: • Practice saying this prayer while making the *Sign of the Cross*.

• Connect the lines to form a solid triangle.

Our Father Prayer
The prayer Jesus taught us.

**Our Father, who art in heaven,
hallowed be thy name.**
(*God is very special. We praise God!*)

**Thy kingdom come;
thy will be done on earth as it is in heaven.**
(*We should obey God's laws.*)

Give us this day our daily bread;
(*We ask God to give us what we need.*)

**and forgive us our trespasses
as we forgive those who trespass against us;**
(*God forgives us when we are sorry.
We should forgive others, too.*)

**and lead us not into temptation,
but deliver us from evil. Amen.**
(*We ask God to help us to be good and to protect us.*)

(Cf. *Mt* 6:9-13)

Discussion:

Jesus prayed often — sometimes alone and sometimes with friends. Jesus wants us to pray and gave us a special prayer to teach us how to pray. This prayer is called the *Lord's Prayer* or *Our Father*. It is said by Christians (friends of Jesus) all over the world.

Activities: • With the help of your teacher and/or parent(s) practice saying the *Our Father*.
• Color the flowers around the prayer.

The Hail Mary

Hail Mary, full of grace,
(Greetings, Mary! God lives in your heart.)

the Lord is with you. Blessed are you among women
(You are God's special friend, and a very special woman.)

and blessed is the fruit of your womb, Jesus.
(You are the mother of Jesus.)

Holy Mary, Mother of God,
(Mary, you are so good. You are the mother of God's Son, Jesus.)

Pray for us sinners,
(Please, ask God to help us be good.)

Now and at the hour of death. Amen.
(Be with us always. Be with us when we're happy, and when we're sad or afraid. Amen.)

Discussion:

This popular prayer begins with two well-known events about Mary found in the Bible. The first is the angel Gabriel's greeting to Mary and telling her about God's great plan — Mary was to become the mother of God's only Son, Jesus! (Cf. *Lk* 1:28) The second is the wonderful greeting Mary received from her cousin Elizabeth. Mary went to visit and help her cousin after learning from the angel Gabriel that Elizabeth was going to have a son, too. (Cf. *Lk* 1:42)

Activities: • With the help of your teacher and/or parent(s) practice saying the *Hail Mary*.
• Color the picture of Mary and the angel Gabriel.

Thank You Prayer

Thank you, God, for creating this wonderful world and for creating me! Amen.

Activity: Color every space that has a heart to highlight the words that you can say for all the wonderful things God created and provides for you every day.

My Own Prayer(s) to God

Activity: • Write your own special prayer(s).
             • Color the picture.